The
DOGS
of
CHICAGO

Susan Curtin

Deborah Schalm

Chicago. Dogs. A Love Affair!

Chicago is a city with a rich and vibrant history, full of fascinating stories and a center of architectural innovation second to none. The city is filled with friendly Midwesterners, who love to explore, exercise and indulge in some of the finest cuisine in the world. I fell in love with Chicago many years ago when I graduated from college and then once again when my daughter was a student at Northwestern.

Having recently moved to Chicago from Greenwich, CT, I discovered hundreds of astounding and remarkable dogs of all shapes, sizes and breeds—many I had never seen before. A new love affair began!

There are few dog walkers in the city, as the majority of owners walk their dogs themselves, enjoying this enviable city life, with so many places to go and people to meet. Such a joy to see! Cycling on the lakefront introduced me to even more gorgeous animals; it was then I knew we had to record these magnificent dogs for the world to know and enjoy. And no matter the weather, Chicago and her dogs shine brightly!

Susan Curtin

Buckingham Fountain

Buckingham Fountain is a Chicago landmark in the center of Grant Park. Dedicated in 1927, it is one of the largest fountains in the world.

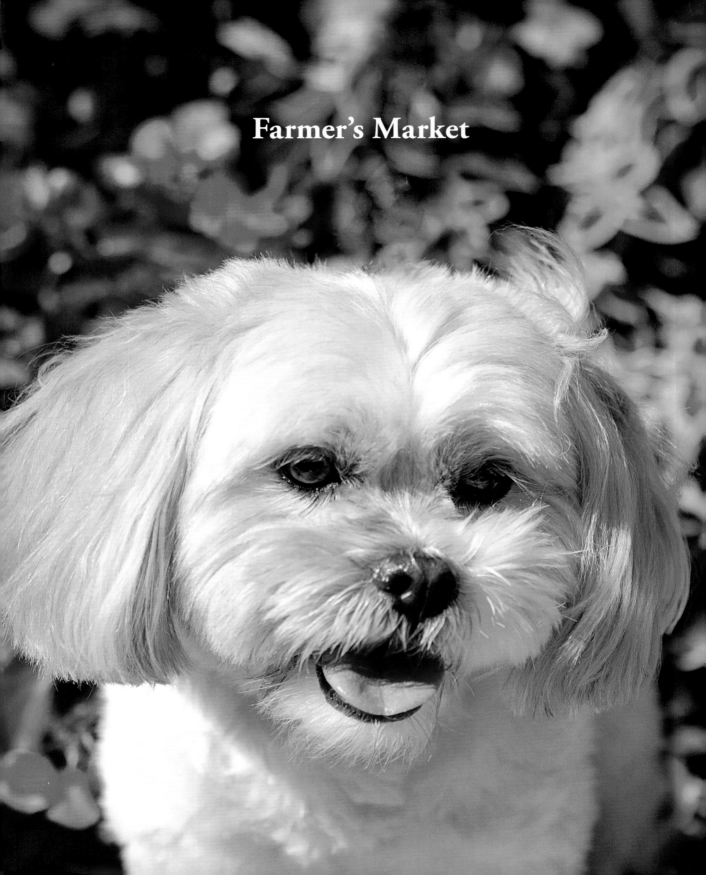

Farmer's Market

The Historic Water Tower

Known for its towers of glass and steel, this is one of Chicago's cherished landmarks. Built by architect William Boyington, construction began in 1867. It was built to conceal a standpipe, which stands 138 feet tall and 3 feet wide. The standpipe served to equalize the water pressure flowing in from the Pumping Station across the street. The design is Gothic and the entire building is 154 feet above ground and was one of the tallest in the world at the time it was built. Besides being a work of art, the choice of materials used in its construction helped it survive the Great Chicago Fire of 1871.

The Original Chicago Tin Man

is a major attraction on the Magnificent Mile!

Navy Pier

Navy Pier, a Chicago landmark, opened to the public in 1916,
it extends nearly one mile out into Lake Michigan. It is among Chicago's
best attractions, a 50-acre playground for all ages. The first Ferris Wheel
made its debut here in 1893.

The Field Museum (above) founded in 1893 has 4.6 million years of history in this vast museum, one of the best in the country, includes Sue, the world's largest T.Rex.

Adler Planetarium (top left) is America's first planetarium and a wonderful resource for all young space explorers.

Shedd Aquarium (bottom left) holds 32,000 fascinating aquatic animals making it one of the largest indoor aquariums in the world.

The Drake Hotel

The Drake Hotel opened in 1920 and during the Roaring Twenties, The Drake Hotel was the first choice for high-society. The Fountain Court, now known as the Palm Court, has continued its daily Afternoon Tea tradition. In 1932 The Cape Cod Room served some of the best fresh fish and seafood and this was the nation's first themed restaurant. In 1933 when prohibition was repealed, Coq d'Or opened and thirsty patrons were able to purchase whiskey. This became a great local hangout for politicians, reporters and true Chicago patrons. The Drake has retained the charm of days gone by.

Dog Beach

Dog Beach at Montrose Harbor is one of the happiest spots in Chicago!
It is an off-leash beach where the dogs run free and love swimming in
Lake Michigan.

George Wellington "Cap" Streeter

was an eccentric resident, showman, aspiring gun runner, squatter and land baron. From the 1880's until his death in 1921 he declared ownership over 186 acres of the most exclusive, prime lakeshore property between the Chicago River and Oak Street, now called Streeterville.

Our Photographer Lucie Burmeister

Dog Breeds

American Pit Bull Terrier
Basset Hound
Beagle
Bernese Mountain Dog
Bichon Frise
Border Collie
Boxer
Bullmastiff
Catahoula Bulldog
Catahoula Leopard
Cavalier King Charles Spaniel
Chow Chow
Dachshund
Dalmatian
Doberman Pinscher
English Bulldog
English Shepherd
Flat Coated Retriever
French Bulldog
German Shepherd

Golden Retriever
Great Dane
Labradoodle
Labrador Retriever
Leonberger
Lhasa Apso
Maltese
Pomeranian
Pug
Saint Bernard
Samoyed
Shar Pei
Shih Tzu
Siberian Husky
Standard Poodle
Weimaraner
West Highland White Terrier
Yorkiepoo
Yorkshire Terrier

Thank You

There are a number of people who were simply amazing in the production of this book. First of all, our lovely and talented photographer Lucie Burmeister. She was a joy to work with, a natural working with the hundreds of dogs—and literally shot many of the photos on her tummy on the ground!

Scott Lander was our very gifted graphic designer. I have worked with Scott on numerous projects and it is always a bundle of fun. He made our dogs come alive in print!

We would like to dedicate this book to all the dog owners. It was our pleasure to work with them and having them share their numerous and amazing stories about their pets.

All the dogs in this book are STARS! But, we have some who we like to call our SUPERSTARS: Aspen, Jagger, Olson, Oliver, Buddy, Scout, Cody, Zac, Callie, Pacer, Dooley, Isabella, Elway, Tristan, Rudy, Lucie, Galipette, Dexter, Wanda, Maximus, Dante, Layla, Diva, Hugo and Kiwi. Thanks!

Note that a portion of the proceeds of this book will be donated to Companions for Wounded Warriors—true SUPERSTARS!

Susan Curtin and Deborah Schalm

ISBN:978-1-5136-1922-4

Printed in Guangzhou, China by PRC Book Printing

First Printing March 2017

thedogsofchicago.com